REVEALING
THE **SPIRIT** OF
GOD

A **50-DAY** PRAYER JOURNEY FOR PENTECOST

CHARISMA
HOUSE

Most CHARISMA HOUSE BOOK GROUP products are available at special quantity discounts for bulk purchase for sales promotions, premiums, fund-raising, and educational needs. For details, write Charisma House Book Group, 600 Rinehart Road, Lake Mary, Florida 32746, or telephone (407) 333-0600.

REVEALING THE SPIRIT OF GOD by Charisma House Editors
Published by Charisma House
Charisma Media/Charisma House Book Group
600 Rinehart Road
Lake Mary, Florida 32746
www.charismahouse.com

Unless otherwise noted, all Scripture quotations are taken from the King James Version of the Bible.

Scripture quotations marked MEV are taken from the Modern English Version. Copyright © 2014 by Military Bible Association. Used by permission. All rights reserved.

Cover design by Lisa Rae McClure
Design Director: Justin Evans

Library of Congress Control Number: 2014957973
International Standard Book Number: 978-1-62136-991-2
E-book ISBN: 978-1-62136-246-5

Portions of this book were previously published by Charisma House as *The Original Maria Woodworth-Etter Devotional*, ISBN 978-0-88419-480-9, copyright © 1997; *The Original John G. Lake Devotional*, ISBN 978-0-88419-479-5, copyright © 1997; *The Original Azusa Street Devotional*, ISBN 978-0-88419-481-1, copyright © 1997; *The Original Smith Wigglesworth Devotional*, ISBN 978-0-88419-482-8, copyright © 1997.

First edition

15 16 17 18 19 — 987654321
Printed in the United States of America

CONTENTS

Part III
Revived by the Spirit

Part IV
Living in the Spirit

INTRODUCTION

You ARE INVITED on a journey to embrace a new and supernatural encounter with the fire and wind of the Holy Spirit that was released on that special Day of Pentecost recorded in Acts chapter 2.

On our modern calendars the Pentecost season is fifty days after Easter, or Resurrection Day, and lasts until the Day of Pentecost. Traditionally this fifty-day period was celebrated as a feast in ancient Israel in remembrance of the giving of the Law of Moses at Mount Sinai. It is still celebrated today in Judaism as Shavuot. In Christendom this time period has come to commemorate the descent of the Holy Spirit upon the one hundred twenty believers waiting for the promise of Christ to be fulfilled: "Wait for the promise of the Father, of which you have heard from Me. For John baptized with water, but you shall be baptized with the Holy Spirit not many days from now" (Acts 1:4–5). This book provides an opportunity for you to take part in the fullness of what those believers experienced.

Our prayer is that you will use this resource in the way that best allows you to receive a deeper understanding of the person of the Holy Spirit. Maybe you will be led to fast during this time. Maybe you will be motivated to read through the Bible's account of the establishment of the early church. And just maybe you will be led to pray for a fresh infilling and revelation of the Holy Spirit as you seek boldness and courage to carry out His will for your life. Whatever the Lord has for you during this time, keep your heart open and your expectations high. He will meet you where you are.

Accompanying you on this journey are the actual words and teachings of great men and women of God such as:

- Maria Woodworth-Etter, who ministered with the power of the Holy Spirit in the nineteenth century. She was one of the first Pentecostal women in America to preach and teach the gospel.

- William J. Seymour, who was the son of ex-slaves but a passionate believer of racial integration. Blind in one eye yet in possession of remarkable vision, Seymour led the Azusa Street Revival in Los Angeles in 1906 and is credited for launching the twentieth-century American Pentecostal movement and several denominations.

- John G. Lake, whose ministry was marked by extraordinary miracles. His writings were anointed and faith-filled.

- Smith Wigglesworth, a powerful prayer warrior whose ministry touched thousands of people in the early part of the twentieth century. Wherever he ministered, miracles, signs, and wonders would follow.

Combined with a daily Scripture verse, points to ponder, and a short prayer, this compilation of some of the most revelatory and Spirit-filled insights into the benefits of Pentecost will bring revival to your heart again and again. You will experience a renewed desire for the supernatural and miraculous empowerment of God's Spirit to work in you and in His church.

So whether the Spirit leads you to fast or feast, we pray that at the end of these fifty days you are drawn into a passionate place, full of zeal and fire for God.

—CHARISMA HOUSE EDITORS

PART I

WAITING FOR
THE SPIRIT

Day 1
THE POWER OF THE HOLY GHOST

Now may the God of hope fill you with all joy
and peace in believing, so that you may abound
in hope, through the power of the Holy Spirit.
[ROMANS 15:13, MEV]

THE LAMB OF God left the realms of glory and came down here to be footsore, dusty, weary, and scorned. He said, "I am come to do Thy will, O God." If He had not borne all these things and had not gone all the way to the cross, the Holy Ghost never could have come. If He had been left in the tomb, the Holy Ghost never could have come. As soon as He arose from the dead and ascended into heaven, the Holy Ghost could come.

God gave His Son the highest place before all the hosts of heaven; then He sent the Holy Ghost to dwell in these bodies, His temple. The Holy Ghost is a great power. He is compared to wind, water, and fire.

At Pentecost He came like a cyclone and a mighty rushing wind. He is to come like rivers of living water. He comes as fire. Tongues of fire sat upon each of the hundred and twenty people at Pentecost. Wind, water, and fire—the most destructive elements we have, yet the most useful.

God uses them to denote the mighty power of the Holy Ghost; and He was to be given after Jesus was glorified. We see many demonstrations of His mighty power, and we can but "speak the things we have seen and heard" of His glory and majesty. When we know these things, we are witnesses to His power, majesty, and glory. Glory to God!

—MARIA WOODWORTH-ETTER

POINTS TO PONDER

- How do you get prepared and prayed up so that you are ready for God's glory in your life?

  - I worship and praise God.
  - I pray in the Spirit and intercede.
  - I spend time reading God's Word and praying.
  - I crucify my flesh and repent daily.
  - Anything else?

By His Spirit, Christ is transforming us "from glory to glory" (2 Cor. 3:18). What is the purpose of this transformation? Read the following verses and write down in your prayer journal how Christ is transforming your life.

  - Colossians 1:9–14
  - Ephesians 1:7–14
  - Galatians 5:2–26
  - Romans 8:1–4

- How are you preparing yourself to receive His glory?

PRAY...

Holy Spirit, come over me like wind, water, and fire. Baptize me in Your power. Amen.

Day 2
SANCTIFIED BEFORE PENTECOST

You are already clean through the
word which I have spoken to you.

[JOHN 15:3, MEV]

B Y READING THE Bible carefully, you can see that the disciples were saved and sanctified men and had received the unction of the Holy Spirit before the Day of Pentecost.

In John 17:15–17, Jesus prays, "I pray not that thou shouldest take them out of the world, but that thou shouldest keep them from the evil. They are not of the world, even as I am not of the world. Sanctify them through thy truth: thy word is truth." Jesus is the Word and the truth, so they were sanctified through the truth the very night that He prayed for them.

Jesus said to the disciples, "Peace be unto you: as my Father hath sent me, even so send I you. And when he had said this, he breathed on them, and saith unto them, Receive ye the Holy Ghost: Whose soever sins ye remit, they are remitted unto them; and whose soever sins ye retain, they are retained" (John 20:21–23).

The disciples were filled with the unction of the Holy Spirit—the anointing—before the Day of Pentecost when Jesus breathed on them. This sustained them until they were endued with power from on high.

In the first chapter of Acts, Jesus taught His disciples to wait for the promise of the Father. This was not to wait for sanctification. His blood had been spilt on Calvary's cross. He was not going to send His blood to cleanse them from carnality but His Spirit to endue them with power. They went up to Jerusalem

3

praising and blessing God with great joy. They all continued with one accord in prayer and supplication.

—WILLIAM J. SEYMOUR

POINTS TO PONDER

- Your personal Pentecost includes your own encounter with the Holy Spirit. Describe how you have encountered the Holy Spirit up to this point.

- Where do you experience the most power in your life?

- Where in your life do you need sanctification?

PRAY...

Jesus, pour out Your Spirit on me, that Joel's prophecy might be fulfilled in my life. Amen.

Day 3
WHY WAIT ON THE HOLY SPIRIT?

But wait for the promise of the Father...For
John baptized with water, but you shall
be baptized with the Holy Spirit.
[ACTS 1:4–5, MEV]

THE DISCIPLES TARRIED at Jerusalem till they were endued with power from on high. We know that the Holy Ghost came. It was right for them to tarry. It is wrong now to wait for the Holy Ghost to come. He has come!

Then why are we waiting? Why do we not all receive the Holy Ghost? Because our bodies are not ready for it. Our temples are not cleansed. When our temples are purified and our minds put in order, then the Holy Ghost can take full charge. The Holy Ghost is not a manifestation of carnality.

The Holy Ghost is most lovely. He is the great refiner. He is full of divine, not natural, life. Don't wait. I desire for you to lift your minds, elevate your thoughts, come out of the world into a place where you know that you have rest for your feet.

Desire the inrushing river of the Holy Ghost—a pure, holy, and divine river of living water to flow through you. Not later. Now!

—SMITH WIGGLESWORTH

POINTS TO PONDER

- Are you ready to receive what those early Christians received at Pentecost? Read the first two chapters of Acts, and then complete these sentences in your prayer journal.

- Jesus promised

- Jesus commanded them to

- In obedience, they

- When the Holy Spirit fell on them, they experienced

- I desire with my heart to

- Have you experienced in your spiritual life what the early Christians experienced? Listed below are some of the characteristics of their experiences. Which of these have you encountered in your own life?

  - Speaking in unknown tongues
  - Filled with the Holy Spirit
  - Operating in the power of the Spirit
  - Praying in the Spirit
  - Boldly witnessing for Christ
  - Miracles
  - Healings
  - Deliverance
  - Joyful giving unto the Lord
  - Hunger for the Word of God
  - Love and unity with other believers

- Which of the items in the list above do you still hunger to receive?

- Write a prayer in your journal, asking God's Spirit for a deep hunger for all that He has for you.

PRAY...

Holy Spirit, purify my heart, my life. Flow in me and through me now. Amen.

Day 4
TARRY IN ONE ACCORD

Suddenly a sound like a mighty rushing
wind came from heaven, and it filled the
whole house where they were sitting.

[ACTS 2:2, MEV]

MAY EVERY CHILD of God seek his real personal Pentecost.
We must stop quibbling and come to the standard that
Jesus laid down for us. Wait on God for this baptism of the
Holy Ghost just now.

Gather two or three people together who are sanctified
through the blood of Christ. Get into one accord, and God will
send the baptism of the Holy Ghost upon your souls as the rain
falls from heaven.

You may not have a preacher to come to you and preach the
doctrine of the Holy Ghost and fire, but you can obey Jesus's
saying in the passage: "Where two or three are gathered together
in my name, there am I in the midst of them" (Matt. 18:20).

This is Jesus's baptism—and if two or three gather together
in His name and pray for the baptism of the Holy Ghost, they
can have it this day or this night, because it is the promise of the
Father. Glory to God!

This was the Spirit that filled the house as a mighty rushing
wind. The Holy Ghost is typified by wind, air, breath, life, and
fire: "And there appeared unto them cloven tongues like as of
fire, and it sat upon each of them. And they were all filled with
the Holy Ghost, and began to speak with other tongues, as the
Spirit gave them utterance" (Acts 2:3–4).

So, beloved, when you get your personal Pentecost, the signs will follow in speaking with tongues as the Spirit gives utterance. This is true. Wait on God, and you will find it a truth in your own life. God's promises are true and sure.

—William J. Seymour

Points to Ponder

- When is Jesus in our midst? Read the following verses, and describe in your journal when He is present:

  - Matthew 18:20
  - Matthew 28:16–20
  - Acts 2:1–2
  - John 14:16–17

- How does Jesus manifest His presence in your midst?

- Revival fell on those gathered in unity under the name of Jesus as they waited for Pentecost. Once we repent and gather in love and unity, the Holy Spirit is free to move sovereignly in our midst. Complete these sentences and write your answers in your prayer journal:

  - When I pray with other believers, the Holy Spirit
  - When believers repent, God's response is
  - Our church will experience revival when

- When do you gather with other believers in unity and love to pray for what God wants to do?

Pray...

Lord, as we gather in one accord waiting upon You, pour out Pentecost and revival upon us. Amen.

Day 5

SPIRIT BAPTISM

But you shall be baptized with the Holy
Spirit not many days from now.

[ACTS 1:5, MEV]

T HE BAPTISM OF the Holy Spirit is power, the understanding
of His Word, and the glory of God upon your life.

Whenever the Lord wants to play His piano, He tunes up the harp and plays with His own fingers, speaking or singing in any language He wishes. The man that hears you speak a message right from the throne falls down and seeks God and gets up to report that God is in you of a truth.

The baptism of the Holy Spirit makes you more humble and filled with divine love. Through Spirit baptism the graces and fruit of the Spirit (Gal. 5:22–23) are manifest.

When you get the baptism with the Holy Ghost, you will surely go up into the mount with Christ. If you want to know what it is to praise God and have the joy of the Lord in your soul that flows like a mighty river, tarry and get your personal Pentecost.

He keeps the rivers flowing in your soul that you may be fit for irrigation wherever you go. Jesus said, "He that believeth on me, as the scripture hath said, out of his belly shall flow rivers of living water. (But this spake he of the Spirit, which they that believe on him should receive…)" (John 7:38–39).

—WILLIAM J. SEYMOUR

POINTS TO PONDER

- Prayer opens the floodgates to the river of God flowing from His throne into your life. Read John 7:38–39 and Revelation 22:1–3. Note all the aspects of God's river that you need to have flowing through your life as you pray.

  - Cleansing
  - Refreshing
  - Renewing
  - Reviving
  - Baptizing
  - Washing
  - Replenishing

- How is the river of God flowing through your life right now?

- Write a prayer in your journal for the specific ways you would like to ask for God's river to flow more freely through you.

PRAY...

Flood me, O Spirit, with Your baptism that Your grace and fruit might be manifested in my life. Amen.

Day 6
THE SPIRIT'S OUTPOURING

"In the last days it shall be," says God, "that
I will pour out My Spirit on all flesh....And
I will show wonders in heaven above."
[ACTS 2:17, 19, MEV]

THIS IS A wonderful scripture, and many do not understand it. There is a certain time spoken of here, when certain great and wonderful things shall take place and people shall know that prophecy is being fulfilled: "It shall come to pass in the last days . . . I will pour out of my Spirit," and there shall be signs in the heavens and the earth—signs of His coming.

This prophecy was first spoken eight hundred years before Jesus came to earth. Peter, standing up on the Day of Pentecost, confirmed it. Under the inspiration of the Holy Ghost, on fire with the Holy Ghost from head to foot, he said these things would come to pass in the last days.

We believe and know by the Word of God and by the signs that we are now living in the last days, the very times Peter spoke about, when we were to know by the mighty things taking place. We are the people, and this is the time just before the notable day of the Lord bursts upon the world. We believe we are the people—yea, we know it.

—MARIA WOODWORTH-ETTER

POINTS TO PONDER

- Three miracles of the Spirit's outpouring are prophecy, dreams, and visions. Read Acts 2:17–21, and then answer these questions.

- When the Spirit outpours, who prophesies?

- Who receives dreams and visions?

- What miracle is seen with the outpouring?

- How have you experienced the outpouring of the Holy Spirit in your life? Complete these sentences and write the answers in your prayer journal:

  - One dream the Spirit has given me is

  - One vision the Spirit has given me is

  - One prophecy the Spirit has given me is

  - A person I have led to Christ is

- How are you encountering the outpouring of His Spirit?

PRAY...

Almighty God, how I rejoice in the outpouring of Your Holy Spirit. Amen.

Day 7
DO NOT STIFLE GOD'S SPIRIT
Do not quench the Spirit.
[1 THESSALONIANS 5:19, MEV]

H E WILL NOT only come in healing power but will manifest Himself in many mighty ways. On the Day of Pentecost, Peter said, "God hath poured forth this which ye see and hear." And from what they heard and saw, three thousand knew it was the power of God and turned to Christ. Others stifled conviction and turned away, saying, "This is the work of the devil."

When the Holy Ghost is poured out, it is either life unto life or death unto death. It is life unto life to those who go forward and death unto death to those who blaspheme against the Holy Ghost. So we want to be careful what we say against the divers operations, supernatural signs, and workings of the Holy Ghost. Some people look on and say, "It looks like hypnotism," or, "I believe it is mesmerism."

To others it appears mere foolishness, even as Scripture says of the natural man, "The natural man receiveth not the things of the Spirit of God: for they are foolishness unto him: neither can he know them, because they are spiritually discerned" (1 Cor. 2:14). Have you received of the life of the Spirit, or are you stifling His conviction?

—MARIA WOODWORTH-ETTER

POINTS TO PONDER

- What God does miraculously can never be discerned in the natural. Only what is spiritual can discern what is of the Spirit. For each Scripture reference listed, write in your prayer journal what that verse says about human wisdom or the revelation of God's wisdom:

- 1 Corinthians 1:27
- 1 Corinthians 1:30
- 1 Corinthians 2:4
- 1 Corinthians 2:5–6
- 1 Corinthians 2:13
- 1 Corinthians 2:14
- 1 Corinthians 2:16

- How are you discerning the spiritual things in your life?
- How are you listening to the voice of the Holy Spirit?

PRAY...

Almighty God, we receive life from You and never want to quench Your Spirit. Amen.

Day 8
FILLED WITH THE SPIRIT

When Paul had laid his hands on them, the
Holy Spirit came on them, and they spoke
in other tongues and prophesied.

[ACTS 19:6, MEV]

THERE IS A necessity for every one of us to be filled with God. It is not sufficient to have just a touch or to be filled with a desire. The only thing that will meet the needs of the people is for you to be immersed in God, so that whether you eat or drink or whatever you do, it may be all for the glory of God. In that place you will find that all your strength, mind, and soul is filled with a zeal, not only for worship, but for proclamation.

That proclamation will be accompanied by all the power of God, which must move satanic power, disturb the world, and make it feel upset.

The reason the world is not seeing Jesus is because Christian people are not filled with Jesus. They are satisfied with weekly meetings, occasionally reading the Bible, and sometimes praying. Beloved, if God lays hold of you by the Spirit, you will find that there is an end of everything and a beginning of God so that your whole body becomes seasoned with a divine likeness of God.

—SMITH WIGGLESWORTH

POINTS TO PONDER

- Being filled with the Spirit means dying to self. Scripture is filled with revelation about dying to selfishness, pride, and self-centeredness. Read the following verses and describe what they say about dying to self.

16

- 2 Chronicles 7:14
- Psalm 51
- Matthew 10:39–42
- Matthew 16:25–26
- Luke 9:24–25
- Luke 17:33
- Romans 12:1–2
- Galatians 2:20
- Philippians 2:1–11
- Philippians 3:7–9

- Have you truly died to self? If not, why not? What keeps you holding on to sin and the past?

  - Fear of losing control
  - Unbelief
  - Desire to continue in past sin
  - Unconfessed sin
  - Ignorance
  - Anything else?

- What will it take for you to surrender all?

PRAY...

Fill me, Holy Spirit. May those people with whom I come into contact daily see only Jesus when they look at my life. Make me a divine likeness of God. Amen.

Day 9
FULLNESS OF THE SPIRIT

For John baptized with water, but
you shall be baptized with the Holy
Spirit not many days from now.

[ACTS 1:5, MEV]

THERE ARE THREE things in life, and I notice that many people are satisfied with only one. There is blessing in justification; in sanctification; and in the baptism of the Holy Spirit.

Salvation is a wonderful thing, and we know it. Sanctification is a process that takes you on to a higher height with God. Salvation, sanctification, and the fullness of the Spirit are processes.

Any number of people are satisfied with "good"—that is, justification or salvation. Other people are satisfied with "better"—that is, a sanctified life, purified by God. Other people are satisfied with the "best"—that is, the fullness of God with revelation from on high.

So I come to you with the fullness of God in the Holy Spirit through His baptism. I come not with good, but better; not with better, but with best.

—SMITH WIGGLESWORTH

POINTS TO PONDER

- Describe how Jesus justified you.
- Describe how Jesus sanctified you.
- Describe the baptism of the Holy Spirit in your life.

PRAY...

Heavenly Father, I thank You for the goodness of Your salvation, the going on with You through sanctification, and the baptism of Your Spirit. Amen.

Day 10
A CONSUMING FIRE

For our God is a consuming fire.
[HEBREWS 12:29, MEV]

GOD'S CALL TO Christian churches today is to come forth from their hiding place, just as Elijah came forth (1 Kings 18), declare the ground on which you meet the enemies of God, and meet them in the name of Jesus Christ.

The time has come when the Christian church must give a new demonstration to the world. If metaphysicians, through the operation of natural laws, can produce a certain character and degree of healing, then it is up to the church of Jesus Christ and the ministers of the Son of God to demonstrate that there is a power in the blood of Jesus Christ to save and heal people unto the uttermost—not half-healed people or half the people healed, but all. I pray and believe that God's time has come for God's challenge to be fulfilled: let the fire fall.

There was no bluffing with the Israelite prophets of old. When the people came, they laid their sacrifices on the altar, and they did not put artificial fire under it. Instead, Elijah bowed down before God. He lifted his heart to heaven, and when the fire came down and consumed the sacrifice, that was the evidence that the sacrifice was accepted.

The time has come when God wants the fire to fall; and if you, my beloved brother and sister, will pay God's price and make Christ's consecration of yourself to God, we will see God's fire fall. And it will not be destructive either, except that sin, selfishness, and sickness will wither under that fire, while purity, life, holiness, and character will stand forth purified and refined by the glory and power of God's fire that comes from heaven—His fire that destroys sin and creates righteousness.

—JOHN G. LAKE

POINTS TO PONDER

- The baptism of the Holy Spirit brings both fire and power. The fire of the Holy Spirit purges, cleanses, and purifies us. Read the following passages about the Spirit's fire, and describe what each reveals about His fire.

    - Isaiah 33:14–16
    - Matthew 3:11–12
    - Luke 3:16–17
    - Acts 1:5, 8
    - Acts 2:1–4
    - 1 Corinthians 3:12–15
    - 1 Peter 1:7–9

- The fire of the Holy Spirit burns away all the dross, wood, hay, and stubble from our lives (1 Cor. 3:12–15). Describe all the impurities in your life right now that the baptizing fire of His Spirit needs to burn away.

- How is the Spirit's baptism of fire purifying you?

PRAY...

Lord, let Your fire fall upon my life, that Your righteousness might shine forth. Amen.

PART II

RECEIVING THE SPIRIT

Day 11
RECEIVE YE THE HOLY GHOST

But the Counselor, the Holy Spirit, whom the Father
will send in My name, will teach you everything.
[JOHN 14:26, MEV]

THE FIRST STEP in seeking the baptism with the Holy Ghost
is to have a clear knowledge of the new birth in our souls,
which is the first work of grace and brings everlasting life to
our souls (Rom. 5:1). Everyone who repents and turns to the
Lord Jesus with faith in Him receives forgiveness of sins. Justification and regeneration are simultaneous. The pardoned sinner
becomes a child of God in justification.

The next step is to have a clear knowledge, by the Holy Spirit,
of the second work of grace wrought in our hearts by the power of
the blood and the Holy Ghost: "For by one offering he hath per-
fected for ever them that are sanctified. Whereof the Holy Ghost
also is a witness to us" (Heb. 10:14–15). We have Christ, crowned
and enthroned in our hearts, the tree of life. We have the brooks
and streams of salvation flowing in our souls, but praise God, we
can have the rivers (John 7:38–39). Christ is now given and being
poured out upon all flesh. All races, nations, and tongues are
receiving the baptism with the Holy Ghost and fire, according to
the prophet Joel (Joel 2:28–32).

When we have a clear knowledge of justification and sanctification through the precious blood of Jesus Christ in our hearts,
then we can be a recipient of the baptism with the Holy Ghost.

—WILLIAM J. SEYMOUR

POINTS TO PONDER

- Do you have a clear knowledge of the new birth in your soul that happened through justification? How would you describe your experience of it?

- Do you have a clear knowledge of the second work of grace, namely your sanctification? How would you describe the experience of sanctification in your life thus far?

- How would you describe your posture toward receiving the Holy Spirit at this point?

PRAY...

Lord, I bow to You, asking You to come into my life, filling and baptizing me with Your Spirit. Amen.

Day 12
THE CYCLONE OF THE SPIRIT

Then the LORD answered Job out of the whirlwind.
[JOB 38:1, MEV]

WE COULD NOT live without fire, wind, or water. When a cyclone comes, men and women turn pale. When God's cyclone through the Holy Ghost strikes the people, it is a great leveler. They lose sight of their money bags. All hatred and ill-will are swept away, as a cyclone carries all before it. When a tidal wave strikes a city, it submerges everything. So, in a tidal wave of the Holy Ghost, everything goes under. Oh, we want a cyclone of God's power to sweep out of our lives everything that cumbers us, and a tidal wave to submerge us in God.

God uses these great elements—fire, wind, and water—in all their force to give us an idea of the mighty power of the Holy Ghost. Our bodies are His temples, and as great pieces of mechanism are moved by electricity, so our bodies, the most wonderful piece of mechanism ever known, are moved by the power of the Holy Ghost sent down from heaven. He filled the one hundred and twenty on the Day of Pentecost with power to witness for Jesus. At the hands of the apostles, God healed the sick, and He heals today by the same power that was on the apostles. God pours out rivers of living waters. What manner of people ought we to be? People living in the cyclone of God's Spirit!

—MARIA WOODWORTH-ETTER

POINTS TO PONDER

- How have you witnessed the Holy Spirit as a cyclone?

- What is it like for you to anticipate the Holy Spirit coming like a cyclone in your life?

- What do you expect would be some specific results of this "great leveler" coming upon your life?

PRAY...

Wind of God, blow in and through my life, moving me in only those directions You would have me go. Amen.

Day 13
SUDDENLY

Suddenly a sound like a mighty rushing
wind came from heaven, and it filled the
whole house where they were sitting.
[ACTS 2:2, MEV]

A T PENTECOST, SUDDENLY they heard a sound like a mighty, rushing wind. This Holy Ghost we are holding up is a mighty power. He came suddenly from heaven, like a windstorm, like floods of water filling the vessels, and as fire upon the heads of one hundred twenty people.

As it were, cloven tongues of fire sat upon their heads. Then the Holy Ghost went in and took possession of the temple. He took full possession of the machinery, wound it up, and set it running for God. They staggered like drunken people and fell. This mighty power took possession of their tongues and spoke through them in other languages.

Away back in the times of the prophets, God said that through men of "stammering lips and another tongue will He speak to this people." Think of that! God's doing such a mighty thing! But some do not want to believe. That is the way the Holy Ghost came and still comes today; and people say it is some other power.

They did not lose their minds; they had just found them! They had the spirit of love and of a sound mind. We never have a sound mind until we get the mind of Christ. People who cannot understand say these things are foolishness. We are told the wisdom of this world is foolishness with God. This is the power and wisdom of God, not the work of the devil; people saying so doesn't make it so.

God had complete control. Suddenly, He came in and took possession. The Holy Ghost is in the world today.

—MARIA WOODWORTH-ETTER

POINTS TO PONDER

- If you had been alive and with those first disciples at Pentecost and spoke in tongues as they did, how would you have responded?

  - Excited or afraid?
  - Bold or timid?
  - Filled with faith or doubtful?
  - Hungering for more or uncertain?

- The same power the disciples experienced during Pentecost is available to you. How might your human reasoning and doubts keep you at arm's length from receiving all God has for you?

- When God took complete control of Samson's life (Judg. 13–16), Samson had miraculous power and strength. When the Spirit came upon him suddenly, he could defeat entire armies of men or pull down the gates of a city. But when Samson took back control of his life, no miracles would happen. What do you need to surrender in order for God's Spirit to take complete control of your life?

- What areas of your life are ready for His complete control?

PRAY...

Suddenly come over me, Holy Spirit, and transform me with Your fire. Amen.

Day 14
THE SPIRIT IN YOU

I will pray the Father, and He shall give you another
Counselor, that He may be with you forever.
[JOHN 14:16, MEV]

THERE IS A difference between the Spirit being in you and the Spirit being with you. For instance, we are getting light now from outside this building. This is exactly the position of every believer that is not baptized with the Holy Ghost. The Spirit is with every person that is not baptized, and they have light from the outside. But suppose all the light that is coming through the window was inside.

That is exactly what is to be taking place. We have revelation from outside, revelation in many ways by the Spirit, but after He comes inside, it is revelation from inside, which will make things outside right.

We are baptizing people in water, remembering that they are put to death, because every believer ought to be covered. Every believer must be put to death in water baptism.

The baptism of the Spirit is to be planted deeper until there is not a part of you that is left. There is a manifestation of the power of the new creation by the Holy Spirit right in our mortal bodies.

Where once we were, now He reigns supreme, manifesting the very Christ inside of us, the Holy Ghost fulfilling all things right there.

—SMITH WIGGLESWORTH

POINTS TO PONDER

- In Acts 2 tongues were a sign for the unbelievers of the miracle-working power of God. They witnessed God's Spirit speaking through Spirit-baptized disciples. The baptism of God's Spirit and the confirming sign of tongues appear elsewhere in Acts. Read the following scriptures and write down how the Holy Spirit confirms His power through tongues.

  - Acts 10:44–46
  - Acts 19:1–7
  - Mark 16:15–18

- The Holy Spirit's baptism brings cleansing fire (Matt. 3:11–12; Luke 3:16–17) and power (Acts 1:8). Describe the baptism of the Holy Spirit in your life.

- What evidences of power from the Spirit are you witnessing in your life?

- Write a prayer asking Jesus to baptize you with the Holy Spirit and fire. If you have already received it, ask Him to refresh your spirit again with His.

PRAY...

Spirit of God, go with me and immerse me with Your living water, that You might reign in all of me. Amen.

Day 15
INTOXICATED BY THE SPIRIT

Do not be drunk with wine, for that is reck-
less living. But be filled with the Spirit.
[EPHESIANS 5:18, MEV]

WHEN YOU ARE intoxicated with the Spirit, the Spirit life
flows through the avenues of your mind and the deep per-
ception of the heart with deep throbbings.

You are so filled with the passion of the grace of God that you
are illumined by the power of new wine—the wine of the kingdom,
the Holy Ghost—till your whole body is intoxicated.

This is rapture! There is no natural body that can stand the
process of this going forth. It will have to leave the body at His
coming. But the body will be a preserver to it until the sons of
God are marvelously manifested.

This holy new life, this preservative of the Son of God in your
human body, this life in you is so after the order of God that it
is not ashamed in any way to say you are coming into co-equality
with the Father, with the Son, and with the Holy Spirit.

—SMITH WIGGLESWORTH

POINTS TO PONDER

- When you think of the word *intoxicated*, what comes to
  mind?

- Have you ever experienced yourself or witnessed another
  person being intoxicated by the Holy Spirit? What was
  that experience like?

- Do you have any fears about being intoxicated by the Holy Spirit? Describe them in your journal.

- Write a prayer that places those fears before God.

PRAY...

Thank You for allowing my life to be filled with the preservative of Your Son's presence within my human body. Fill and intoxicate me, O Holy Spirit, that I might live and move in You. Amen.

Day 16
LET THE SPIRIT WORK IN YOU

You shall receive power when the Holy Spirit
comes upon you. And you shall be My witnesses.
[ACTS 1:8, MEV]

MANY PEOPLE TEACH today that no one has the Holy Spirit until he is baptized with the Holy Ghost. The Holy Ghost comes in different degrees, such as the filling of the Spirit and the baptism in the Spirit. The baptism comes down on your head like a cloud.

When the prophets were anointed, the oil was poured over their heads, and then the Holy Ghost came into them. The Holy Ghost must come upon our heads and then all through us, taking possession of us. Many people do not think of anything but speaking in tongues. They lay everything else aside.

Thirty-five years ago I was baptized with the Holy Ghost and fire, and I stood alone. When the Pentecostal movement broke out, some said they would not have anything but tongues, so I was kept back. I could not do much with the movement at first. There was so much false teaching that the Holy Ghost was driven away from many people. They wanted the Holy Ghost to work this way and not that way. Let the Holy Ghost work in any way that agrees with the Word of God.

—MARIA WOODWORTH-ETTER

POINTS TO PONDER

- When you think of the baptism in the Spirit, what comes to mind?

- How do you respond to the idea that the Holy Spirit's

manifestation through a person might look different from you expect?

- On a scale of one to ten, with ten being very open, how open are you to the Holy Spirit working in and through you in ways you've never experienced before?

- In what ways has the Holy Spirit worked in you or those around you in ways you never expected?

PRAY...

Holy Spirit, move in my life in whatever way You desire, that I might be Your vessel to glorify the name of Jesus. Amen.

Day 17
RECEIVE AND REVEAL
GOD'S POWER

God worked powerful miracles
by the hands of Paul.
[ACTS 19:11, MEV]

THE HUMAN BEING is God's marvelous, wonderful instrument. You and I are the most marvelous and wonderful creatures in all God's creation in our capacity to receive and reveal God. Paul received so much of God into his being that when people brought handkerchiefs and aprons to him, his touch impregnated those articles with the loving Spirit of God, the living substance of God's being. The effect was that when these articles were laid upon those who were sick or possessed of devils, the Word says they were healed by God (Acts 19:11–12).

We have been so in the habit of putting Jesus or the apostles in a class by themselves. As a result, we have failed to recognize that Jesus made provision for the same living Spirit of God that dwelt in His own life, and of which He was a living manifestation, to inhabit our lives, just as the Spirit inhabited the beings of Jesus or Paul.

The fact that people brought to Paul handkerchiefs and aprons and these articles became impregnated with the Spirit and people were healed when they touched them is a demonstration that any material substance can become impregnated with the same living Spirit of God.

—JOHN G. LAKE

POINTS TO PONDER

- Are there ways that you set Jesus and the apostles in a class apart from you and what can happen today? What are some specific ways you do this?

- What kind of openness are you being invited to have toward these things instead?

- What kind of power would you like to see the Holy Spirit demonstrate through you and/or others?

PRAY...

Lord Jesus, so fill me with Your Spirit that my life becomes impregnated with the same living Spirit that healed the sick through You. Amen.

Day 18
GOD'S FIRE IS STILL FALLING

I indeed baptize you with water to repentance, but
He who is coming after me is mightier than I....He
will baptize you with the Holy Spirit and with fire.

[MATTHEW 3:11, MEV]

THE WAVES OF Pentecostal salvation are still rolling in at
Azusa Street Mission. From morning until late at night the
meetings continue, usually with three altar services a day. We
have kept no record of souls saved, sanctified, and baptized with
the Holy Ghost, but a brother said last week he counted about
fifty in all that had been baptized with the Holy Ghost during
the week. Then at Eighth Street and Map Avenue, the People's
Church, Monrovia, Whittier, Hermon, Sawtelle, Pasadena, Ely-
sian Heights, and other places, the work is going on and souls are
coming through amid great rejoicing.

Four of the Holiness preachers have received the baptism with
the Holy Ghost. One of them, Brother William Pendleton, with
his congregation being turned out of the church, is holding meetings at Eighth Street and Maple Avenue. There is a heavenly atmo-
sphere there. The altar is filled with seekers. People are slain under
the power of God and are rising up in a life baptized with the
Holy Ghost.

The fire is spreading. People are writing from different points
to know about this Pentecost and are beginning to wait on God.

He is no respecter of persons and places. We expect to see a
wave of salvation go over this world. While this work has been
going on for five years, it has burst out in great power on this
coast. There is power in the full gospel. Nothing can quench it.

—WILLIAM J. SEYMOUR

POINTS TO PONDER

- Have you ever witnessed the falling of the Holy Spirit like the one described above? If so, what was it like? If not, how do you think you would respond if it happened?

- What is your posture toward the possibility of this kind of activity of God happening where you live?

- How do you think such an outbreak of the Spirit would affect your own daily life and activities?

PRAY...

Jesus, baptize me with Your fire, that I might be consumed with passion for You. Amen.

Day 19
TONGUES CONVICT SINNERS

Are not all these who are speaking Galileans? How is it that we hear, each in our own native language?
[ACTS 2:7–8, MEV]

THE POWER OF the Holy Spirit was greatly manifested in our meetings by the speaking in unknown tongues. This was much criticized by the town and vicinity, so the principal physician, who was familiar with several different languages, was prevailed upon to go to the meetings in order to denounce them as a fake. Miss Tuthill, in an unknown language to herself but known to the doctor as Italian, spoke his full name, which no one in the town knew save himself, telling him things that had happened in his life twenty years ago and on up to the present time, until he cried for mercy and fell on his knees seeking God.

He found full salvation the next day and is now a believer in the gospel that Jesus taught and also in the power of the Holy Ghost that was given unto us to witness to a living Christ. That physician now says he would rather pray for the sick than give drugs and is seriously thinking of leaving his profession and going into the Lord's work.

Many precious souls have been saved, sanctified, and baptized with the Holy Ghost as a result of the preached Word under the Spirit's anointing.

—CHARLES PARHAM

Points to Ponder

- The greatest miracle witnessed in the early church was salvation. Salvation resulted as the gospel was preached in boldness and the fear of God brought repentance to the lost. Before miracles are manifested, the fear of God and repentance must be present in the church. Read the following scriptures and write down in your prayer journal what they say to you about repentance.

  - Matthew 4:17
  - Acts 2:38
  - Acts 3:19
  - 2 Corinthians 7:10

- The life of the early church was filled with the presence of the Holy Spirit, who performed signs and wonders in their midst. Survey the first five chapters of the Book of Acts. List in your prayer journal ten evidences of the power of the Holy Spirit that were manifested in the early church.

- Circle the manifestations evident in your church today in the list above.

- What miracles are being manifested in your life?

Pray...

Spirit of God, speak to my heart, that I may be convicted of sin and set free to serve You totally. Amen.

Day 20
RECEIVING THE HOLY GHOST

When He had said this, He breathed on them
and said to them, "Receive the Holy Spirit."
[JOHN 20:22, MEV]

GOD HAS TOLD His children to be witnesses, and the most convincing evidence is testimony of personal knowledge.

I dropped into the meetings on Azusa Street some time in April, having heard that some people were speaking in tongues as they did on the Day of Pentecost.

At first the meeting seemed a very tame affair to me. As I was indoctrinated in the second blessing being the baptism with the Holy Ghost, I branded the teaching as heretical, not going to the meetings for some time.

In fact, I could not stay away. My heart began to break up, and soon I was going from one person to another, asking them to forgive me for harsh words and criticism.

I began to earnestly seek for the Lord to have His way with me. The Holy Ghost showed me that I must be clay in the Potter's hands, an empty vessel before the Lord.

On a Saturday morning I awoke and stretched my arms toward heaven and asked God to fill me with the Holy Ghost. My arms began to tremble, and soon I was shaken violently by a great power. About thirty hours afterwards, while sitting in the meeting on Azusa Street, I felt my throat and tongue begin to move without any effort on my part. Soon I began to stutter and then out came a distinct language which I could hardly restrain.

—G. A. COOK

POINTS TO PONDER

- In what way can you relate to this author's experience of first branding something as heretical but then being unable to stay away?

- Do you know others who are in that position right now? Name them in your prayer journal.

- Write out a prayer in your journal on behalf of the people you named and the work God is seeking to do in their lives.

PRAY...

Spirit of God, fill me with Your baptism of tongues, fire, joy, and laughter. Amen.

Day 21
SIGNS OF THE HOLY GHOST

These signs will accompany those who believe.
[MARK 16:17, MEV]

MANY PEOPLE TODAY have an intellectual faith and a historical faith. They believe. Well, the devils believe and tremble. Belief is one thing, but faith is another. "The letter killeth; the Spirit giveth life." If the truth is hid, it is hid to those who are lost.

We may have intellectual imaginations, go through a course of study, and learn the doctrines of men. However, no one but the Holy Ghost can give us knowledge of "the things of God." They seem foolishness to the natural man. Sometimes the Holy Ghost gives a spirit of laughter and sometimes one of weeping, with everyone in the place being affected by the Spirit.

I have stood before thousands of people and could not speak, just weep. When I was able to see, people were weeping everywhere. That is one way the Holy Ghost works. I have stood for an hour with my hand raised, held by the mighty power of God. When I came to myself and saw the people, their faces were shining.

God moves in mysterious ways His wonders to perform. He is the God I worship. Jesus says, "Behold I and the children which God hath given me" (Heb. 2:13). We believe in signs and wonders, not from beneath but from above. We are a people to be wondered at. We are a sign among the people.

—MARIA WOODWORTH-ETTER

POINTS TO PONDER

- When the power of the Holy Spirit comes upon you, how are you affected by His miracle-working power? List in your journal all that apply to you.

  - I am changed.
  - I am renewed and revived.
  - I weep with repentance.
  - I weep for joy.
  - I laugh.
  - I dance.
  - I shout.
  - I sing unto the Lord.
  - I worship and praise Him.
  - I fall down in His presence.
  - I shake and tremble in His presence.
  - Anything else?

- Read Acts 4. Look for all the changes in the early believers wrought by the power of the Holy Spirit. List in your prayer journal the changes that you observe. Circle any changes that you personally need to make in your own spiritual life.

- What miraculous changes has Christ made in your life this past week?

- What changes does He still need to make?

PRAY...

Lord, through Your power, make of me a sign to others, pointing to You. Amen.

Day 22
EXPERIENCING GOD'S POWER

For to those who are perishing, the preaching
of the cross is foolishness, but to us who
are being saved it is the power of God.

[1 CORINTHIANS 1:18, MEV]

IN THE BIBLE we read how men fell when they caught a glimpse of God's glory. Paul tells us there are those who have a form of godliness but deny the power thereof; from such we are to turn away. "In the last days perilous times shall come," and those who have reprobate minds shall withstand God's children to their faces, even as the magicians withstood Moses.

In the last days, there will be some people living very near to God; but the devil will have his workers, too, who will attribute signs and wonders done to any power except the power of Christ. The Lamb of God, the Lion of the tribe of Judah, has never lost His power and never will lose His power. I would hate to say, by my actions, that I thought the devil had more power than God.

There is a wonderful difference between the power of God and any of those other powers. The Holy Ghost comes only in Christ. He only comes into the bodies of those who love God. When He takes possession of us, He takes us away into the sweetest experience this side of heaven—that of being alone with God. He talks to us and reveals to us "things to come" (John 16:13).

It is wonderful! God puts us under the power, and God takes us out. No man can bestow this power upon another. It comes only through Jesus Christ. There are two kinds of power, and people who do not know the difference will stand up today and say that wisdom is foolishness.

—MARIA WOODWORTH-ETTER

POINTS TO PONDER

- The power of God changes us into the image of Christ, while the power of this world destroys us and brings destruction and death into our lives. Read Galatians 2:20 and 2 Corinthians 3:18. Then write all the ways the Spirit is conforming you to the image of Christ by His power.

- The two kinds of power are God's power and the world's counterfeit power. God's power changes us and gives true life. Read 2 Corinthians 5:17. Describe how the miracle-working power of God has changed your life and made you a new creation.

- How are you being changed in Christ?

- What in you still needs to be changed by Christ?

PRAY...

Holy Spirit, take possession of me, that I might know the sweetest experience this side of heaven. Amen.

Day 23
THE TRUE PENTECOST

Greater is he who prophesies than
he who speaks in tongues.

[1 CORINTHIANS 14:5, MEV]

W E CAN HAVE all the nine gifts as well as the nine fruits
of the Spirit, for in Christ Jesus dwells all the fullness of
the Godhead bodily. Paul is simply teaching the church to be in
unity and not to be confused because all have not the same gifts.

We are not confused because one has his Pentecost and
another has not been sanctified. We do not say that we do
not need the justified or the sanctified brother simply because
he does not speak with tongues or does not prophesy. But
we realize that it takes the justified, the sanctified, and the
Pentecost brother all to make up the body of Christ.

You may have the gift of wisdom, healing, or prophecy, but
when you get the Pentecost, the Lord God will speak through
you in tongues.

"Greater is he that prophesieth than he that speaketh with
tongues, except he interpret." The brother that prophesies is no
greater than the brother that speaks in tongues if the brother
interprets as he speaks. We have a good many here that interpret as they speak, and it is edifying. The gifts are for you if you
will only ask the Lord for them.

In 1 Corinthians 14, Paul is setting us in order that have the
baptism with the Holy Ghost and the speaking in tongues, that
we should not get puffed up. In getting into deep spiritual things
and into the hidden mysteries of God, people have to keep very

humble at the feet of the Lord Jesus, for these precious gifts can easily puff us up if we do not keep under the blood.

—WILLIAM J. SEYMOUR

POINTS TO PONDER

- Below is a list of the gifts of the Spirit. What gifts have you seen manifested in your life now?

  - Wisdom
  - Knowledge
  - Faith
  - Healing
  - Prophecy
  - Discernment
  - Tongues (unknown languages)
  - Interpretation of tongues (unknown languages)
  - Miracles
  - Teaching
  - Helping others
  - Apostleship
  - Serving others
  - Encouraging
  - Ability to lead
  - Giving generously
  - Kindness
  - Evangelism
  - Pastoring
  - Preaching

- Which gifts are you praying will come into your life for full ministry to flow through you?

- Complete the following sentences and write the answers in your prayer journal:

  - I praise God for stirring these gifts up in me:

  - I am tempted to become prideful when God gifts me to

  - One way I resist pride when ministering in the gifts is

- When others minister with gifts you have not experienced, how do you feel?

PRAY...

Jesus, I seek You above the gifts. Give me those gifts You desire, that I may minister Your grace to others. Amen.

PART III

REVIVED BY THE SPIRIT

Day 24
PENTECOSTAL REVIVAL

Many signs and wonders were performed among
the people by the hands of the apostles. And
they were all together in Solomon's Porch.
[ACTS 5:12, MEV]

THIS WAS THE greatest revival given in the New Testament—
greater in many ways than Pentecost. Then they were all
with one accord and in place while awaiting the outpouring of
the Spirit. You get there, and God will shake the country.

Signs and wonders were wrought, and of the rest dare no
man join himself unto them. They were so full of fire no person
dared say falsely, "I am one of you." They were afraid God would
strike them dead.

God wants to get a people so full of His power that others
full of wildfire will say, "God, fill me with the real power."

What was the result of Pentecost? Believers were added to
the church? No, they were added to the Lord, both men and
women. Some say that this excitement and fanaticism is good
enough for women, but there was also a multitude of strong-
minded men there.

They brought the sick into the streets and laid them on
beds and couches so that Peter's shadow might overshadow
some of them. See what a cranky set they were! I wish we were
just like that. Excitement rose higher and higher. The whole
country was stirred. There came multitudes from the city of
Jerusalem, bringing the sick, and they were healed. Why?
Because they came seeking God and not man. A wonderful
revival, was it not?

—MARIA WOODWORTH-ETTER

POINTS TO PONDER

- What brings revival? Read Acts 1–2, and then list all the things in your prayer journal that brought revival to the disciples.

- Read 2 Chronicles 7:14 and Acts 3:19. How does revival come to God's people through prayer?

- Describe what God needs to do in your life in order to bring revival to you, enabling His signs and wonders to be manifested in your life.

PRAY...

Lord, send Your revival to the church and to me. Amen.

Day 25
THE HOLY GHOST IS POWER

My speech and my preaching was not with enticing words of man's wisdom, but in demonstration of the Spirit and of power.

[1 CORINTHIANS 2:4, MEV]

THERE IS A great difference between a sanctified person and one that is baptized with the Holy Ghost and fire. A sanctified person is cleansed and filled with divine love, but the one that is baptized with the Holy Ghost has the power of God on his soul and has power with God and men, power over all the kingdoms of Satan and over all his emissaries.

In all Jesus's great revivals and miracles, the work was wrought by the power of the Holy Ghost flowing through His sanctified humanity. When the Holy Ghost comes and takes us as His instruments, this is the power that convicts men and women and causes them to see that there is a reality in serving Jesus Christ.

Oh, beloved, we ought to thank God that He has made us the tabernacles of the Holy Ghost. When you have the Holy Ghost, you have an empire, a power within yourself.

The Lord never revoked the commission He gave to His disciples: "Heal the sick, cleanse the lepers, raise the dead" (Matt. 10:8). Jesus is going to perform these things through us if He can get a people in unity.

Jesus said, "Behold, I give unto you power to tread on serpents and scorpions, and over all the power of the enemy" (Luke 10:19).

—WILLIAM J. SEYMOUR

POINTS TO PONDER

- In revival, the power of the Holy Spirit is manifested. How? Through the baptism of the Spirit, signs, wonders, salvations, and miracles. Read the following passages from Acts, and describe all the different ways you observe the Spirit moving in power:

  - Acts 2:1–7
  - Acts 2:41–47
  - Acts 3:1–11
  - Acts 4:1–4
  - Acts 4:23–37
  - Acts 5:1–11
  - Acts 5:12–16
  - Acts 6:7–8

- What signs and wonders are you witnessing in your life and church? Has revival arrived, or is it still anticipated? What of the following evidences of the power of the Holy Spirit have you witnessed recently in your life and church? Write them in your prayer journal.

  - Healings
  - Miracles
  - Deliverances
  - Salvations
  - Manifestations of the gifts
  - The baptism of the Holy Spirit

- Signs and wonders
- Repentance
- Powerful prayer
- Anything else?

- What will it take for revival to break out in your church?
- What will it take for revival to break out in you?

PRAY...

Through me, Lord, heal the sick, cleanse the lepers, raise the dead, cast out devils, and freely use all I have to minister. Amen.

Day 26
SPREAD THE FIRE

For by one Spirit we are all baptized into
one body, whether we are Jews or Gentiles,
whether we are slaves or free, and we have
all been made to drink of one Spirit.

[1 Corinthians 12:13, mev]

When Brother William Pendleton and thirty-five of his members were turned out of the Holiness church, they were invited by Brother Bartleman and other workers to occupy the church at Eighth Street and Maple Avenue. It had just been opened up for Pentecostal work. And God has been using them as never before.

When some of the saints were rejected from the Nazarene church at Elvsian Heights on account of the baptism with the Holy Ghost and evidence of tongues, they opened cottage prayer meetings where hungry souls flocked.

> Truth crushed to earth will rise again.
> The eternal years of God are hers;
> But error wounded writhes in pain,
> And dies among its worshippers.

In California, where there has been no unity among churches, they are becoming one against this Pentecostal movement. But, thank God, the source is from the skies and cannot be cut off from below. The dear church people know not what they do. Many of them are hungry and coming and saying, "This is just what I have been longing for, for years."

God is drawing His people together and making them one. No new church or division of the body of Christ is being formed. Christ never had but one church. We may be turned out of the big wood-and-brick structures, but "by one Spirit are we all baptized into one body" (1 Cor. 12:13).

—WILLIAM J. SEYMOUR

POINTS TO PONDER

- Pentecost came when the first followers and disciples of Jesus were meeting together in one accord—unity. How unified is the body of Christ where you worship? How unified is the body in your town or city?

- What can you do to bring more unity to the body of Christ? Name at least one thing and write out your thoughts in your prayer journal.

- How can churches work together to win the lost where you live?

PRAY...

Lord God, make us one as the Father and the Son are one, that we might dwell in the unity of the Spirit. Amen.

Day 27
PRAYING FOR THE HOLY GHOST

If you then, being evil, know how to give good gifts to your children, how much more will your heavenly Father give the Holy Spirit to those who ask Him?
[LUKE 11:13, MEV]

W E ARE NOW hearing from individuals and companies who are definitely waiting on God for their personal Pentecost. Some have been stimulated in seeking by hearing of God's visitation in Los Angeles. We join hands with all such hungry seekers and meet you at the throne.

Before another issue of this paper, we look for Brother Parham in Los Angeles, a brother who is full of divine love and whom the Lord raised up five years ago to spread this truth. He, with other workers, will hold union revival meetings in Los Angeles and then expects to go on to other towns and cities and will appoint workers to fill the calls that come in.

Begin to pray right away for a revival in your neighborhood or town or city. Perhaps you need one in your own closet or at your family altar first. But expect great things from God. Begin to prepare for a revival—a great and deep revival—and believe for it. It may cost you money, and it may humble you, but prepare for the Lord's coming.

—WILLIAM J. SEYMOUR

POINTS TO PONDER

- Who is praying and working for revival in the land?

- Without prayer, revival cannot come. Without working the harvest, revival cannot come. Read 2 Chronicles 7:14

62

and Luke 10:2, and summarize what these verses teach about prayer and harvest.

- What personal sacrifices are you willing to make to see revival come? In your prayer journal, write each action that you are willing to take:

  - Give money sacrificially and cheerfully.

  - Pray without ceasing.

  - Fast unto the Lord.

  - Witness and work in the harvest.

  - Serve the saints while they work in the harvest.

  - Be trained and equipped to witness and disciple others.

  - Anything else?

- Revival is rooted in prayer, repentance, and a surrender that is willing to do whatever God asks. How willing are you to pay the cost of revival? What holds you back?

PRAY...

God, send revival to my life, my family, and my town. Revive me that I might be a torch to revive others. Amen.

Day 28
RIVERS OF LIVING WATER

He who believes in Me, as the Scripture has said,
out of his heart shall flow rivers of living water.
[JOHN 7:38, MEV]]

IN THE FOURTH chapter of John, the words come: "Jesus answered and said unto her, If thou knewest the gift of God, and who it is that saith to thee, Give me to drink; thou wouldest have asked of him, and he would have given thee living water" (v. 10). Praise God for the living waters today that flow freely, for they come from God to every hungry and thirsty heart.

We are able to go in the mighty name of Jesus to the ends of the earth and water dry places, deserts, and solitary places until these parched, sad, lonely hearts are made to rejoice in the God of their salvation. We want the rivers today.

In Jesus Christ we receive forgiveness of sins, sanctification of our spirit, soul, and body, and upon sanctification we may receive the gift of the Holy Ghost that Jesus promised to His disciples, the promise of the Father. All this we get through the atonement. Hallelujah!

The prophet said that Jesus had borne our griefs and carried our sorrows: "He was wounded for our transgressions, he was bruised for our iniquities: the chastisement of our peace was upon him; and with his stripes we are healed" (Isa. 53:5). We have healing, health, salvation, joy, life—everything in Jesus. Glory to God!

—WILLIAM J. SEYMOUR

Points to Ponder

- Jesus teaches the woman at the well—and us—the importance of living water. We cannot survive spiritually without the Spirit's flow of living waters into our lives. How is the spiritual river flowing within you?

  - Being refreshed in the Spirit or stale in the Spirit?
  - Dry and thirsty or filled with the Spirit?
  - Free in the Spirit or hindering the Spirit?
  - Overflowing with the Spirit or stagnant in the Spirit?

- Note your answers in your prayer journal.

- True revival flows in the river of God. His living water flows through His people and refreshes anyone who is thirsty for God. How is the river of God flowing in your life? In your church?

- The living water of God in revival brings healing. Read Revelation 22:1–2. In your prayer journal, rewrite the passage in your own words.

- In what ways have you been healed by His living water?

Pray...

Thank You, Jesus, for the living water that flows from Your throne into my life, filling me with salvation, healing, and revival. Amen.

Day 29
WORDS THAT SHAKE THE WORLD

My speech and my preaching was not with
enticing words of man's wisdom, but in demonstration of the Spirit and of power.

[1 CORINTHIANS 2:4, MEV]

PAUL SAID HIS teaching "was not with enticing words of man's wisdom, but in demonstration of the Spirit and of power." That shakes the world, and it is just the same today. You say you do not like this power. Well, the devil does not like it either. I have been out in the work for thirty-five years, and people fell under the power by thousands before I preached healing.

There were mighty outpourings of the Spirit that made the devil howl. It shows how little we know of the real gospel when we take the letter of the law. It is like skimmed milk. No man can understand the deep things of God except by the Spirit.

Paul had much knowledge, but he said the wisdom of this world was foolishness in the sight of God. True wisdom comes from heaven. The Word must be preached in simplicity. Jesus had the eloquence of high heaven at His command, yet He used language that the most uneducated could understand.

—MARIA WOODWORTH-ETTER

POINTS TO PONDER

- Are you experiencing the miracle-working power of God in your life and church? If not, then a form of godliness or human religion and tradition may be hindering the power of God. Human reason cannot decipher and understand God's miracles. Read 1 Corinthians 1:18–2:16, and then complete the following sentences in your prayer journal.

- Human wisdom cannot

- The ways in which God's wisdom is manifested are

- Spiritual things are understood by

- Believers have

- What forms of godliness tempt you to deny the power of God?

- Human ways and traditions stifle the power of the Holy Spirit. Paul writes, "Quench not the Spirit" (1 Thess. 5:19). Remove from your life anything unholy or rooted in a form of godliness that quenches the Spirit's power. (See 2 Corinthians 7:1.) Read 1 Thessalonians 4:1–12, and then write a prayer repenting of anything in your life that would quench the Spirit.

PRAY...

Jesus, give me words to declare with simplicity Your gospel. Amen.

Day 30
THE HOLY SPIRIT QUICKENS

But if the Spirit of Him who raised Jesus from the dead lives in you, He…will also give life to your mortal bodies through His Spirit that lives in you.
[ROMANS 8:11, MEV]

MANY PEOPLE ARE receiving a clear knowledge of an inward working power from the Spirit which is not only quickening their mortal bodies, but also pressing into that natural body an incorruptible power which is manifesting itself, getting ready for the rapture.

It is the inward life, the new man in the old man, the new nature in the old nature, the resurrection power in the dead form, the quickening of all, the divine order of God manifested in the human body that quickens us, giving us life. The nature of the living Christ gives us power over all death.

Do not be afraid to claim the quickening, life-giving power of the Holy Spirit. That is power over all sin, power over all disease.

The former law was of the natural man. Now the new law is of the life of the Spirit or the manifestation of the new creation, which is Christ in us, the manifested power of the glory. Glory is a manifestation of a divine nature in the human body.

—SMITH WIGGLESWORTH

POINTS TO PONDER

- One manifestation of the Spirit's moving in revival is healing. God heals, delivers, saves, and sets us free when

He moves in power. Write down what the Word reveals about His healing.

- Exodus 15:26
- Psalm 103:3
- Psalm 107:20
- Jeremiah 17:14
- Mark 6:13
- James 5:14–15

- God revives us physically, emotionally, mentally, and spiritually with His healing power. Do you need His healing? Complete the following sentences, and write the answers in your prayer journal.

  - I need His physical healing for

  - I need His emotional healing for

  - I need His intellectual healing for

  - I need His spiritual healing for

- How are you praising God for your healing before you see it?

PRAY...

Holy Spirit, quicken my body with Your divine nature and glory. Amen.

Day 31
WIND, PERSON, AND FIRE

He who believes in Me, as the Scripture has said,
out of his heart shall flow rivers of living water.

[JOHN 7:38, MEV]

JESUS SPOKE ABOUT the Holy Ghost which was to be given. In Acts 2 we find three manifestations of the Holy Ghost—wind, person, and fire. The first manifestation is a rushing mighty wind. Second, there are cloven tongues of fire. Think of the mighty wind and the cloven tongues of fire over everyone. Third, see the incoming and outflowing of the Holy Ghost.

Can we be filled with this river? How is it possible for us to flow as a river?

You will never get to know God better by testimony. Testimony should always come through the Word. You will not get to know God better by prayer. Prayer has to come out of the Word. The Word is the only thing that reveals God and is going to be helpful in the world. When the breath and the presence of God come, the Holy Spirit speaks expressively according to the mind of the Father and the Son.

When you are filled with the person of the Holy Ghost, then the breath, the power, the unction, the fire of the Spirit takes hold of the Word of Life, which is Christ. God wants to fill you with that divine power so that out of you will flow living waters.

—SMITH WIGGLESWORTH

POINTS TO PONDER

- How would you describe your thirst for God's living water right now?

- What have you experienced of God's living water in the past?

- In your prayer journal, write a prayer for the living water of God to flow through you regarding a specific situation in your life right now.

PRAY...

May the fire, wind, and person of the Holy Spirit fill me, that out of me will flow living waters so that others might know Jesus through me. Amen.

PART IV

LIVING IN THE SPIRIT

Day 32
THE BAPTISM'S REAL EVIDENCE

If I speak with the tongues of men and of
angels, and have not love, I have become
as sounding brass or a clanging cymbal.

[1 CORINTHIANS 13:1, MEV]

T HE REAL EVIDENCE that a man or woman has received the
baptism of the Holy Ghost is divine love, which is charity.
That person will have the fruit of the Spirit.

"But the fruit of the Spirit is love, joy, peace, longsuffering,
gentleness, goodness, faith, meekness, temperance: against such
there is no law. And they that are Christ's have crucified the
flesh with the affections and lusts" (Gal. 5:22–24).

The fruit of the Spirit is the real Bible evidence in their daily
walk and conversation. The outward manifestations of the Spirit's
baptism are speaking in tongues and signs following: casting out
devils; laying hands on the sick and the sick being healed; and the
love of God for souls increasing in their hearts (Mark 16:15–18).

—WILLIAM J. SEYMOUR

POINTS TO PONDER

- The fruit of the Spirit is the character of Christ being
  formed in us, while the gifts and manifestations of the
  Spirit are the ministry of Christ as He works through us.
  Copy the following list of the fruit of the Spirit in your
  prayer journal. In front of each fruit write a number from
  one to ten to indicate the degree to which the gift has
  matured and manifested in your life (with ten being very
  much matured and manifested).

75

- Love
- Goodness
- Joy
- Faith
- Peace
- Meekness
- Long-suffering
- Temperance
- Gentleness

- What outward manifestations of the fruit have you experienced in your own life or in your church? Note them in your prayer journal.

  - Casting out devils
  - Laying hands on the sick and seeing them healed
  - Speaking in tongues
  - Signs and wonders
  - Love for souls
  - Anything else?

- Love is seeking God's best for another person. To whom do you need to demonstrate God's love today? List three people by name and describe how you will show them God's love.

PRAY...

Lord, grow Your fruit in my life. Amen.

Day 33
SPEAKING IN TONGUES

And they were all filled with the Holy Spirit
and began to speak in other tongues, as
the Spirit enabled them to speak.

[ACTS 2:4, MEV]

T HE HOLY GHOST is a wonderful person, not a myth or
shadow. Pentecost, when the Holy Ghost came in to stay, is
the greatest thing that ever happened in God's work. He came
and took possession of one hundred twenty men and women;
He sat upon their heads in cloven tongues of fire. He took possession of their bodies; then of their vocal organs; and they
spoke, everyone, as He gave them utterance.

They spoke in languages they had never learned and did not
know what they were saying. The Holy Ghost took possession
of their tongues and spoke through them; He spoke through
the clay as you would speak through a telephone and told about
Jesus. "He shall testify of Me."

Jesus told the apostles that they should be witnesses. When
the Holy Ghost came, He knew all about it, and through the
apostles He told of the wonderful works of God. When this
was noised abroad, multitudes gathered. It was the speaking in
tongues that drew the people. When the people heard the apostles, they were confounded and said, "What meaneth this?"

I want you to notice this point—it was speaking in tongues
that confounded them. The Holy Ghost spoke through these
unlearned men who had never been to college to learn other

77

languages. It was one of the most wonderful things God ever did. It is now, when God speaks through you.

—MARIA WOODWORTH-ETTER

POINTS TO PONDER

- How has the Holy Spirit taken over your tongue?

- How is that which comes out of your mouth your own thoughts and flesh?

- What is your experience with the gift of tongues?

- Read Romans 1:16–17. Then, in your prayer journal, paraphrase it in your own words.

PRAY...

Holy Spirit, take possession of my tongue. Speak through me as You did those early Christians. Amen.

Day 34
GOD'S POWER CANNOT BE BOUGHT

Peter said to him, "May your money perish
with you, because you thought you could
purchase the gift of God with money!
[ACTS 8:20, MEV]

PREACH IN A simple way, and demonstrate. The seal is put upon the Word by the Holy Spirit. Many say that when we lay hands upon the people, they get mesmerized. I am sorry they do not know more of the power of God. There was a great revival at Samaria. Simon the sorcerer was baptized, but none of them had been baptized with the Holy Ghost. Peter and John went to Samaria and laid hands on them, and they received the Holy Ghost.

Simon recognized the power was different from sorcery, and he wanted it. He offered them money to give him this power, that whomsoever he laid hands on might receive the Holy Ghost. The apostles were horrified. They said, "Thy money perish with thee, because thou hast thought that the gift of God may be purchased with money" (Acts 8:20).

The Holy Ghost and His power are gifts of God. No one can buy them. Many people today do not understand any more than Simon did.

By the laying on of the apostles' hands, something happened: the Holy Ghost fell on those people, and they had great blessing.

—MARIA WOODWORTH-ETTER

POINTS TO PONDER

- Simon had the wrong motivation for giving. Read the following verses, and write down what the Bible says about giving.

  - Matthew 6:19–24
  - Mark 12:41–44
  - Luke 6:38
  - 2 Corinthians 8:7–9
  - 2 Corinthians 9:6–7

- When you give to the Lord, how do you feel, and what is your attitude?

  - Expecting something in return
  - Joyful
  - Grateful to God
  - Seeking future reward
  - Loving God
  - Desiring to please God
  - Anything else?

- What parts of your life still need to be totally yielded to the Lord? Why do you struggle to give them to Him?

PRAY...

Lord, I seek the power of the Holy Spirit, not for my glory but for Yours. Amen.

Day 35
THE MINISTRY OF THE HOLY SPIRIT

But the manifestation of the Spirit is given
to everyone for the common good.
[1 CORINTHIANS 12:7, MEV]

THE PROFESSIONAL MINISTRY does not want the gifts today. Christians are baptized with the Holy Ghost so that the whole body may be edified.

The working of the Holy Ghost is the visible sign of the presence of Jesus. They went from Jerusalem to preach the gospel, and the Lord was with them. I love that word. He is in heaven—but He is also with us.

The Lord was with them, confirming the Word. How? With signs and wonders following. Wherever they went they saw faces shine, someone healed, someone speaking in tongues. This you see and hear—it is the Holy Ghost—and it is for the work of the ministry. We do not need professional ministers. Everyone filled with the Holy Ghost can minister in the gifts.

I have tested the truth; I know it is of God. How can we help talking of the things we have seen? I have seen things by the Spirit and in visions. I have seen Jesus, the heavens open, the marriage supper, hosts of angels, the glory of God. I have seen them, glory to God! I know what I am telling you. I know Jesus lives and is standing by my side more truly than I know you are here. These things are verities.

I am not ashamed of the gospel of Christ. Glory to God! When a weak woman comes here to tell you what strong men in the ministry ought to have told you, what are you going to think about it? I say these things are true; and when people say they are foolishness and fanaticism, dare they attempt to prove it by the Word? I dare them to do it.

—MARIA WOODWORTH-ETTER

POINTS TO PONDER

- Read 1 Corinthians 12:1–11, and list in your prayer journal the nine gifts mentioned there. Then circle the gifts that are operating in your life.

- Which of the gifts above do you desire the Spirit to manifest through you? Write a prayer to the Spirit asking for that gift.

- Are you bold for Christ or simply lukewarm? Rate where you are right now. List the number in your prayer journal for each item that best represents your relationship with Christ from one (cold) to five (hot).

  - My love for Christ
  - My boldness in witnessing to others
  - My hunger for His presence
  - My zeal to know Him more and more
  - My desire to fellowship with His sufferings
  - My commitment to serve Him

PRAY...

God, give me boldness to minister with the Spirit's gifts, no matter what. Amen.

Day 36
THE MINISTRY OF THE SPIRIT

Now we have received not the spirit of the world,
but the Spirit which is of God, so that we might
know the things that are freely given to us by God.
[1 CORINTHIANS 2:12, MEV]

THE MINISTRY OF the Christian is the ministry of the Spirit. He not only ministers words to another, but he ministers the Spirit of God. It is the Spirit that inhabits the words, speaks to the spirit of another, and reveals Christ in and through him.

In the old days when I was in Africa, I would walk into the native meetings when I did not understand the languages and would listen to the preacher for an hour, not understanding a word he said. But my soul was blessed by the presence of the Spirit.

Perhaps I had heard better words than his, perhaps clearer explanation of the Scriptures than he could give, but I was blessed by the presence of God.

The ministry of the Christian is the ministry of the Spirit. If the Christian cannot minister the Spirit of God, in the true sense he is not a Christian. If he has not the Spirit to minister, in the highest sense he has nothing to minister. Other men have intellectual knowledge, but the Christian is supposed to be the possessor of the Spirit.

A minister of Jesus Christ is as far removed above the realm of psychological influences as heaven is above the earth. He ministers God Himself into the very spirits, souls, and bodies of people.

—JOHN G. LAKE

POINTS TO PONDER

- The Holy Spirit has inspired within you mighty gifts
  for ministry that can only be released through prayer.
  Through prayer, the Spirit communicates God's will
  for ministry and releases power to use His gifts. What
  are those gifts released by prayer? Read the following
  scriptures and list in your prayer journal the gifts they
  mention.

  - Romans 12:5–8

  - 1 Corinthians 12

  - Ephesians 4:7–16

  - 1 Peter 4:10–11

- Look over the list that you have just written. Circle all the
  gifts that you have used in ministry. Underline every gift
  that has been ministered to you. The church is built up as
  we minister to one another and pray in the Spirit.

- Read Jude 20, and then rewrite it in your own words.

PRAY...

*Spirit of God, use me to minister Your life to others.
Amen.*

Day 37
STIR UP THE GIFT IN YOU

Therefore I remind you to stir up the gift of God,
which is in you by the laying on of my hands.
[2 TIMOTHY 1:6, MEV]

P AUL HAD SOME faith in the value of the putting on of his
hands. It was not a mere form. I want to call your attention
to the Word of God especially on this line. Paul's own convictions were that through laying on of hands upon this young man,
an impartation of God to his life had been given.

It was so real that even though Timothy was not aware of
it and was not exercising the power of God thus bestowed, yet
Paul's conviction was that the power of God was present. Why?
Because he had laid his hands on Timothy in the name of the
Lord Jesus Christ, and he believed the Spirit of the Lord Jesus
Christ had been imparted to Timothy. Therefore the gift of God
was in him.

Beloved, it takes faith to exercise your gift of God. There are
just lots of people around everywhere who have gifts of God, and
they are lying dormant in their lives, and there is no value for
the kingdom of God through them because they have no faith in
God to put the gift in exercise and get the benefit of it.

Too many preachers are afraid of the devil. They have no idea
how big God is. They preach fear of the devil, fear of demons,
fear of this influence, fear of that influence, and fear of some
other power. If the Holy Ghost has come down from heaven
into your soul, common sense teaches that He has made you the
master thereby of every other power in the world. Otherwise

the Word of God is a blank falsehood. For it declares, "Greater is he that is in you, than he that is in the world" (1 John 4:4).

—JOHN G. LAKE

POINTS TO PONDER

- Read 2 Timothy 1:6–7. In your own words, describe what Paul tells Timothy about the ministry gift that he has.

- What gifts does the Spirit desire for you to use in ministering to the body?

- In your journal, write a prayer asking God to reveal to you the gifts He desires to stir up within you.

PRAY...

Lord, give me the courage to use the gift that You have put in me. Amen.

Day 38
HE THAT IS IN YOU

He who is in you is greater than
he who is in the world.
[1 JOHN 4:4, MEV]

GOD ANOINTS YOUR soul. God anoints your life. God comes to dwell in your person. God comes to make you a master. That is the purpose of His indwelling in a Christian. The real child of God was to be a master over every other power of darkness in the world. The world was to be subject to him. He is to be God's representative in the world.

The Holy Ghost in the Christian was to be as powerful as the Holy Ghost was in Christ. Indeed, Jesus's words go to such an extreme that they declare, "Greater works than these shall he do" (John 14:12). It indicates that the mighty Holy Ghost from heaven in the life of the Christian was to be more powerful in you and in me after Jesus got to heaven and ministered Him to our souls than He was in Jesus.

Fear of the devil is nonsense. Fear of demons is foolish. The Spirit of God anointing the Christian heart makes the soul impregnable to the powers of darkness.

"God hath not given us the spirit of fear; but of power, and of love, and of a sound mind" (2 Tim. 1:7). The Spirit of power is the Holy Ghost, bless God. And not only of power, but of love and of a sound mind. Not a craziness and insanity, but a sound mind, by which you can look in the face of the devil and laugh.

—JOHN G. LAKE

POINTS TO PONDER

- What is like for you to hear that the Holy Spirit is meant to be as powerful in you as He was in Christ?

- Where does fear show up in your life right now?

- If you were to imagine your life without fear in it, how would things be different?

- In your journal write a prayer asking God to help you in the specific ways you struggle with fear.

PRAY...

Lord, I thank You that the Holy Spirit gives me power over the devil and all his demons. Amen.

Day 39
SPEAK IN THE SPIRIT

I thank my God that I speak in
tongues more than you all.
[1 CORINTHIANS 14:18, MEV]

Paul desired for all to speak in tongues. Yet he said that in the church he would rather speak five words with understanding, that by his voice he might teach others, than ten thousand words in an unknown tongue. He urged us not to forbid one another to speak with tongues (1 Cor. 14:39).

Tongues are one of the last signs of the soon return of Jesus. For all that are baptized with the Holy Ghost, the first words they speak in an unknown tongue, when interpreted, are "Jesus is coming soon; get ready." Everyone that speaks in an unknown tongue should pray that he might interpret.

Paul said, "Desire spiritual gifts." He that speaks in an unknown tongue speaks unto God. No man understands him, but in the Spirit he speaketh mysteries. He edifies himself, but if he interprets or someone else interprets, he edifies the whole church.

Tongues are for a sign to unbelievers that Jesus is coming soon and that the Holy Ghost is poured out. Those who have the gift of tongues can speak at will or any time that the Spirit is moving. Some even lose their experience and still speak at any time, anything they want to, casting reflections on the cause of Christ. Speaking in tongues without the power of the Holy Ghost is done in the flesh and is not of God.

—MARIA WOODWORTH-ETTER

POINTS TO PONDER

- What is your experience with tongues?

- What is your experience with the interpretation of tongues?

- How open is your church to these gifts?

PRAY...

God, empower me to speak by Your Spirit and not of my flesh. Amen.

Day 40
HONOR THE HOLY GHOST

Do not quench the Spirit. Do not
despise prophecies. Examine all things.
Firmly hold onto what is good.
[1 THESSALONIANS 5:19–21, MEV]

HONOR THE HOLY Ghost. Do not quench the Spirit. It is not you that speaks but the Holy Ghost, and He will speak when He chooses.

Don't you ever try to speak with tongues or say that the power belongs to you. It is "'by my spirit,' saith the LORD" (Zech. 4:6). He wants you to pray for the interpretation so that you can speak with the Spirit and with the understanding also (1 Cor. 14:15).

—WILLIAM J. SEYMOUR

POINTS TO PONDER

- How do we know if the spiritual power being manifested is truly from God or counterfeit? First John teaches us how to test the spirits. Read 1 John 4:1–10 and complete the following sentences in your prayer journal.

  - The Spirit of God confesses

  - Other spirits not from God do not

  - Greater is

  - Love is manifested when

- Why do some people oppose the Spirit of God working miracles today? In your prayer journal, note all the reasons you have observed for their opposition.

- Fear
- Unbelief
- Rebellion
- Anger at God
- Lack of understanding
- Intellectual reasoning against miracles
- Hurts because God did not respond to past needs
- Anything else?

- When you encounter worldly power and opposition to God, what is your response?

- In your prayer journal, write a prayer asking God for the power to discern the spirits of this world.

PRAY...

I honor You, Holy Spirit, with my thoughts, words, and actions. Amen.

Day 41
HIS SPIRIT IN US

But the manifestation of the Spirit is given
to everyone for the common good.
[1 CORINTHIANS 12:7, MEV]

G OD HAS PRIVILEGED us in Christ Jesus to live above the
ordinary human plane of life. Those who want to be
"ordinary" and live on a lower plane can do so; but as for me,
I will not!

We have the same God that Abraham and Elijah had. We
need not come behind in any gift or grace. We may not possess
the abiding gifts, but if we are full of the Holy Ghost and divine
unction, it is possible, when there is need, for God to manifest
every gift of the Spirit through us to give a manifestation of the
gifts as God may choose to use us.

This ordinary man Stephen became mighty under the Holy
Ghost's anointing. He stands supreme in many ways among
the apostles.

"And Stephen, full of faith and power, did great wonders and
miracles among the people" (Acts 6:8). Stephen was just as ordinary as you and me, but he was in the place where God could
so move upon him that he, in turn, could move all before him.
He began in a most humble place and ended in a blaze of glory.
Beloved, dare to believe in Christ!

—SMITH WIGGLESWORTH

POINTS TO PONDER

- Read Acts 6–7, and then complete the following sentences in your prayer journal.

- One way my faith is like Stephen's is

- One way I am not like Stephen is

- If I faced dying for Christ, I would

- To die for Jesus would be

- What words best describe Stephen's miraculous faith? Write in your prayer journal all the words you believe best describe his wonder-working faith:

  - Bold
  - Courageous
  - Assured
  - Dynamic
  - Unafraid
  - Sharp
  - Convicting
  - Real
  - Anything else?

- What needs to happen in your life for your faith to be like Stephen's?

- What miracles might happen in your life if you were more like Stephen?

PRAY...

Holy Spirit, empower me to go beyond the ordinary to the extraordinary through Your power and unction. Amen.

Day 42
SANCTIFIED BY THE SPIRIT

Elect according to the foreknowl-
edge of God the Father, through sanctification by the Spirit, for obedience and
sprinkling with the blood of Jesus Christ.

[1 PETER 1:2, MEV]

THERE IS A sanctifying of the human spirit. It does not matter what you say, if your human spirit does not get wholly sanctified, you will always be in danger. It is that position where the devil has a chance to work on you.

Therefore, we are taught to come into sanctification, where the rudiments, the uncleanness, the inordinate affections and corruptions pass away because of incorruption abiding. In sanctification, all kinds of lusts have lost their power.

This is the plan. Only in the ideal pursuit of this does God so bless us in our purifying state that we lose our earthly position and ascend with Him in glory. The saints of God, as they go on into perfection and holiness, understanding the mind of the Spirit and the law of the Spirit of life, are brought into a very blessed place—the place of holiness, the place of entire sanctification, the place where God is enthroned in the heart.

The sanctified mind is so concentrated in the power of God that the saint thinks about the things that are pure and lives in holy ascendancy, where every day he experiences the power and liberty of God.

—SMITH WIGGLESWORTH

POINTS TO PONDER

- To be sanctified means "to be set apart and made holy by the Holy Spirit." Read 2 Corinthians 7:1; 1 Thessalonians 4:3; and 1 Peter 3:15, and then summarize in your prayer journal what you must do in sanctification.

- Now read the following verses and summarize what Christ has done and is doing to sanctify us.

  - John 17:19
  - 1 Corinthians 1:30
  - Ephesians 5:26
  - 1 Thessalonians 5:23
  - 2 Thessalonians 2:13

- How is Christ sanctifying you now?

PRAY...

Sanctify me, Holy Spirit, that I may be filled with You, not me. Amen.

Day 43
WALK AND LIVE IN THE SPIRIT

That the righteous requirement of the law
might be fulfilled in us, who walk not according
to the flesh but according to the Spirit.

[ROMANS 8:4, MEV]

WE MUST KNOW that the baptism of the Spirit immerses us into an intensity of zeal, into a likeness to Jesus, to make us into pure, running metal, so hot for God that it travels like oil from vessel to vessel.

This divine line of the Spirit will let us see where we have ceased and He has begun. We are at the end for a beginning. We are down and out, and God is in and out.

There isn't a natural thought of any use here. There isn't a thing that is carnal, earthly, natural that can ever live in a meeting.

No man is able to walk spiritually without being in the Spirit. He must live in the Spirit.

He must realize all the time that he is growing in the same ideal of his Master, in season and out of season, always beholding the face of the Master, Jesus.

—SMITH WIGGLESWORTH

POINTS TO PONDER

- There is no power apart from a personal relationship with Jesus Christ. We repent, are obedient in baptism, and receive the gift of the Holy Spirit (Acts 2:38). In the Spirit is all power to live eternally and to live a life filled with signs and wonders. Read the following scriptures,

and write down the power available to you as a child of
God through faith in Christ.

- Acts 1:8
- Romans 15:13
- 2 Corinthians 12:9
- Ephesians 1:18–21
- Ephesians 3:20
- Philippians 3:10
- Colossians 1:10–11

- What blocks the power of God in your life? As God's child,
  His miracle-working power (*dunamis*) is available to you at all
  times and in all situations. But hindrances can arise to block
  that power and thus impede miracles in your life. Write in
  your prayer journal any of the hindrances listed below that
  may presently be blocking God's power in your life.

  - Unconfessed sin
  - Pride
  - Rebellion
  - Unbelief
  - Disobedience
  - Anything else?

- How is the Spirit's power flowing freely and without hin-
  drance in your life?

PRAY...

Holy Spirit, immerse me, that Your zeal will run hot in my life for Jesus Christ. May I never stop growing more and more Christlike through Your power. Amen.

Day 44
THE LIFE OF THE SPIRIT

Joshua…and Caleb…spoke to all the assembly of
the children of Israel, saying…"Do not fear them."
[NUMBERS 14:6, 7, 9, MEV]

THE SPIRIT WAS so mighty upon Joshua and Caleb that
they had no fear. The Holy Spirit upon them had such a
dignity of reverence to God that these two people brought the
bunches of grapes and presented them to the people. There
were ten people sent out. They had not the Holy Spirit and
came back murmuring.

I am speaking about people who get the Holy Ghost and go on
with God, not about the people who remain stationary.

I pray that the same Holy Spirit on Joshua and Caleb will
fill you and search your hearts. Be filled with the life of the
Spirit that we call unction, revelation, and force. What do
I call force? Force is that position in the power of the Spirit
where, instead of wavering, you go through. Instead of judg-
ment, you receive truth.

—SMITH WIGGLESWORTH

POINTS TO PONDER

- Read Numbers 13–14. What is your impression of Joshua
  and Caleb?

- How does your faith mirror theirs?

- In what areas does your faith need to grow in greater likeness to theirs?

PRAY...

Holy Spirit, fill me with Your boldness and power to go on with You and not to waver or murmur. Amen.

Day 45
PRAYING AS THE SPIRIT PRAYS

But the Spirit Himself intercedes for us
with groanings too deep for words.
[ROMANS 8:26, MEV]

WE MUST HAVE life in everything. Who knows how to pray but as the Spirit prayeth? What kind of prayer does the Spirit pray? The Spirit always brings to your remembrance the mind of the Scriptures and brings forth all your cry and your need better than your words. The Spirit always takes the Word of God and brings your heart, and mind, and soul, and cry, and need into the presence of God.

So we are able to pray only as the Spirit prays, and the Spirit only prays according to the will of God, and the will of God is all in the Word of God. No man is able to speak according to the mind of God and bring forth the deep things of God out of his own mind.

Now I can see that the Holy Ghost so graciously, so extravagantly puts everything to one side that He may ravish our hearts with a great inward cry after Jesus.

—SMITH WIGGLESWORTH

POINTS TO PONDER

- How have you experienced the intercession of the Holy Spirit in your life?

- What are some ways you can make greater room for the Holy Spirit's intercession?

- In your journal write out a prayer to the Holy Spirit concerning His intercession on your behalf.

PRAY...

Holy Spirit, ravish my heart. Set aside all distractions. Pray through me that my heart's cry might be heard in the presence of God. Amen.

Day 46
THE SPIRIT PRAYS IN US

We do not know what to pray for…but
the Spirit Himself intercedes for us.
[ROMANS 8:26, MEV]

How DO YOU come to God? Where is God? Is He in the air? In the wind? He that cometh to God, where is He? God is in you. Oh, hallelujah! And you will find the Spirit of the living God in you, which is the prayer circle; which is the lifting power; which is the revelation element; which is the divine power that lifts you.

He that cometh to God is already in the place where the Holy Ghost takes the prayers and swings them out according to the mind of the Spirit. For who hath known the mind of Christ, or who is able to make intercession but the mind of the Spirit of the living God? Where is He? He is in us!

God answers prayers because the Holy Ghost prays; your advocate is Jesus; and the Father is the judge of all. There He is. Is it possible for any prayer to miss on those lines?

—SMITH WIGGLESWORTH

POINTS TO PONDER

- Where are some concrete places you have experienced the presence of God?

- How do you experience the presence of God inside you?

- What does it mean for you to have the mind of Christ?

PRAY...

Spirit of God, pray in me, through me, and in spite of me. Amen.

Day 47
THE HOLY SPIRIT

Jesus returned in the power of the Spirit.
[LUKE 4:14, MEV]

IF WE STUDY the manner by which the Spirit of God revealed Himself through Jesus, then we will have the pattern or example of how the Spirit of God reveals Himself through all believers all the time.

Through His nature there flowed a subtle power that no religionist but Himself and His followers possessed—the living Spirit of the living God, the anointing of the Holy Ghost.

So long as Christianity is dependent on the presence of the Holy Ghost, it will remain distinctively the one religion of divine power and saving grace.

—JOHN G. LAKE

POINTS TO PONDER

- How did the Spirit of God reveal Himself through Jesus?

- What does this mean about the way the Spirit of God wants to reveal Himself through you?

- How have you witnessed the "subtle power" of the living Spirit of God at work in yourself and others?

PRAY...

Holy Spirit, my life depends totally on You. Amen.

Day 48
CLEANSED BY THE SPIRIT

Such were some of you. But you were washed,
you were sanctified, and you were justified in the
name of the Lord Jesus by the Spirit of our God.

[1 CORINTHIANS 6:11, MEV]

THE SPIRIT NEVER comes to a man's life to whitewash him
over or smooth him over or clean him up. God comes to
him to make him new and give him a new heart. God gives him
a new mind, a new spirit, new blood, new bone, and new flesh.

God's Spirit sends him out with a new song in his mouth
and a new shout of praise in his heart and a new realization of
holiness—a truly redeemed man.

—JOHN G. LAKE

POINTS TO PONDER

- What does *new* mean to you?

- How have you experienced yourself made new in God?

- In what areas of your life are you in need of newness?

- In your prayer journal, write a prayer for that specific
  kind of newness you long to receive.

PRAY...

*God, fill us by Your Spirit, and send us forth among
men—not whitewashed, but washed white with Your
grace. Amen.*

Day 49
THE FEAST OF PENTECOST

There appeared to them tongues as of fire,
being distributed and resting on each of them,
and they were all filled with the Holy Spirit.

[ACTS 2:3–4, MEV]

THE FEAST OF Pentecost is the very type of the baptism with the Holy Ghost. The word *Pentecost* signifies fifty days. The first Pentecost the Jews had was at Mount Sinai fifty days after the feast of Passover.

The baptism with the Holy Ghost also fell on Pentecost just fifty days after Jesus was offered on the cross. The regular time of offering the lamb of sacrifice was nine o'clock, and that was the hour that Jesus was crucified—the third hour of the day. And the baptism of the Spirit fell at the same hour, fifty days later.

In the second chapter of Acts, we read that Peter said to the multitude, "These are not drunken, as ye suppose, seeing it is but the third hour of the day" (v. 15).

The Pentecost fell on the Lord's Day, the first day of the week, or Sunday. It has been kept by God's people ever since. Pentecost really means a feast; praise God, we have Pentecost today.

The feast of Pentecost came at the time of the wheat harvest and ripening of the summer fruits. They were commanded to leave some of the wheat and fruits in the fields, not to glean it. When we get the baptism with the Holy Ghost, we have overflowing love, we have rivers of salvation. Praise our God.

—WILLIAM J. SEYMOUR

POINTS TO PONDER

- What is your experience of celebrating the Feast of Pentecost?

- In what way would you consider Pentecost a feast? What are its similarities to an actual feast?

- Pentecost came in the fullness of time—when the harvest was come and the summer fruits had ripened. In what way are you witnessing the fullness of time around you and/or in your own life?

PRAY...

O God, pour out Your Pentecost in my life. Amen.

Day 50
PENTECOST

But when the Counselor comes, whom I shall send to you from the Father, the Spirit of truth who proceeds from the Father, He will bear witness of Me.

[JOHN 15:26, MEV]

HE IS THE Holy Ghost. The Lord speaks of the Holy Ghost as a person as much as He would of one of the apostles. On the Day of Pentecost, they were all of one accord, in one place, and something happened.

It will happen every day if you have the Spirit. "Suddenly there came a sound from heaven as of a rushing mighty wind." This was the Holy Ghost when He came to stay. "There appeared unto them cloven tongues like as of fire, and it sat upon each of them. And they were all filled with the Holy Ghost, and began to speak with other tongues, as the Spirit gave them utterance" (Acts 2:3–4).

When this was noised abroad, multitudes came together. What was noised abroad? That these people were all speaking in other languages. The news went through Jerusalem, and the multitude came together and were confounded because every man heard them speak in his own language. Those who came were men out of every nation under heaven.

They heard these hundred and twenty speak in their own language wherein they were born. This is what gathered the people and confounded them. "They were all amazed and marvelled, saying one to another, Behold, are not all these which speak Galileans? And how hear we every man in our own tongue, wherein we were born?...We do hear them speak in our tongues the wonderful works of God" (Acts 2:7–8, 11).

—Maria Woodworth-Etter

Points to Ponder

- How have you witnessed Pentecost in your life experience?

- Today, what is your prayer concerning the gift of the Holy Spirit?

- How can you celebrate the gift of the Holy Spirit in your life today?

Pray...

Fire of the Holy Ghost, fall on me, that I might speak in other tongues and testify of the mighty and wonderful works of God. Amen.